Understanding the Texas Constitution

Jason Steinagle

New York

Published in 2014 by The Rosen Publishing Group, Inc.
29 East 21st Street, New York, NY 10010

Copyright © 2014 by The Rosen Publishing Group, Inc.

Book Design: Jonathan J. D'Rozario

Photo Credits: Cover Aaron Price/Shutterstock.com; p. 5 Yellow Dog Productions/Lifesize/Getty Images;
p. 7 http://en.wikipedia.org/wiki/File:Scene_at_the_Signing_of_the_Constitution_of_the_United_States.jpg;
p. 9 (White House) Vacclav/Shutterstock.com; p. 9 (Supreme Court) Mustafa Dogan/Shutterstock.com; p. 9
(Capitol) Orhan Cam/Shutterstock.com; p. 10 PAUL J. RICHARDS/AFP/Getty Images; p. 11 Scott Olson/Getty
Images News/Getty Images; p.12 http://en.wikipedia.org/wiki/File:Galveston_Federal_Building_2009.jpg; p.14
http://en.wikipedia.org/wiki/File:Edmund_Davis.jpg; p.15 TIM SLOAN/AFP/Getty Images; p.17 Dave Hughes/
E+/Getty Images; p.19 spirit of america/Shutterstock.com; p. 21 Blanscape/Shutterstock.com; p. 23 Fort Worth
Star Telegram/McClatchy-Tribune/Getty Images; p. 24 Eric Gay/AP Images; p. 25 Witold Skrypczak/Lonely Planet
Images/Getty Images; p. 26 http://en.wikipedia.org/wiki/File:TexasSupremeCourtBuilding.JPG; p. 27 SAUL LOEB/
AFP/Getty Images; p. 29 Warren Price Photography/Shutterstock.com.

Library of Congress Cataloging-in-Publication Data

Steinagle, Jason R.
Understanding the Texas Constitution / by Jason R. Steinagle.
  p. cm. — (Spotlight on Texas)
Includes index.
ISBN 978-1-4777-4542-7 (pbk.)
ISBN 978-1-4777-4543-4 (6-pack)
ISBN 978-1-4777-4541-0 (library binding)
1. Texas — Politics and government — Juvenile literature. 2. Texas — Juvenile literature. I. Title.
F386.S84 2014
976.4—d23

Manufactured in the United States of America

CPSIA Compliance Information: Batch #WW14RC: For further information contact Rosen Publishing, New York, New York at 1-800-237-9932.

CONTENTS

GOVERNMENTS IN TEXAS

Texas's government is modeled after the U.S. federal government. Both were founded on principles laid out in their constitutions. While there are many similarities between the Texas Constitution and the U.S. Constitution, there are also important differences. The governments they established also have important similarities and differences.

The purpose of both the federal and Texas governments is to serve and protect citizens through the three branches of government established in their constitutions—legislative, executive, and judicial. The legislative branch makes laws. The executive branch **enforces** laws. The judicial branch interprets the laws, or decides what they mean. Citizens elect many members of these branches on the state and federal levels, reflecting the idea of popular sovereignty. This means the people of Texas, like all people in the United States, decide for themselves who will represent them in their government.

> The Texas and the U.S. Constitutions reflect the principle of republicanism. This is the belief in a government where people have the power to choose their leaders.

Roots in the Ancient World

The Founding Fathers of the United States found inspiration in the governments of ancient Greece and Rome. In Greek democracy, citizens could vote on all issues. Rome also gave citizens a say in government, but in a different way. The system that worked well in the small Greek city-states wasn't practical in the large territory ruled by Rome. So Rome created something called a republic, in which citizens elect representatives to govern and make laws for them. The values of both ancient Greece and Rome can be seen in the U.S. government and the governments of each state, including Texas.

U.S. Constitution Basics

The first U.S. government was established through the Articles of Confederation, which were **ratified** on March 1, 1781. The Articles created a weak national government, giving most of the power to the states. Many Americans feared a strong national government would take away their individual rights and leave them no better off than they were under England's rule. As years passed, though, the Founding Fathers realized America needed a stronger federal government. In 1787, a convention was called in Philadelphia to amend the Articles of Confederation. The **delegates** soon realized a new constitution was needed.

The U.S. Constitution was ratified on June 21, 1788. It established the separation of powers between the three branches of the federal government, and it divided power between the federal government and the states. On December 15, 1791, the Constitution was amended to include the Bill of Rights. These first 10 amendments list individual rights given to all U.S. citizens, including religious freedom, the right to bear arms, and the right to a fair trial.

Texas wasn't represented at the Constitutional Convention of 1787 because it belonged to Spain at that time. It didn't become a state—and, therefore, didn't adopt the U.S. Constitution—until 1845.

Changing the Constitution

The amendment process for the U.S. Constitution has two parts—proposal and ratification. A proposal for an amendment must be approved by either two-thirds of Congress or two-thirds of state **legislatures**. Once the proposal has been approved, three-fourths of the states must ratify the amendment.

Not all constitutional amendments work. The 18th Amendment, introduced to the U.S. Senate by Texan John Morris Sheppard and passed in 1919, made the sale of alcohol illegal in the United States. As a result of this amendment, crime rose as people illegally made and sold alcohol. Then, the 21st Amendment was passed in 1933, allowing people to sell alcohol once again.

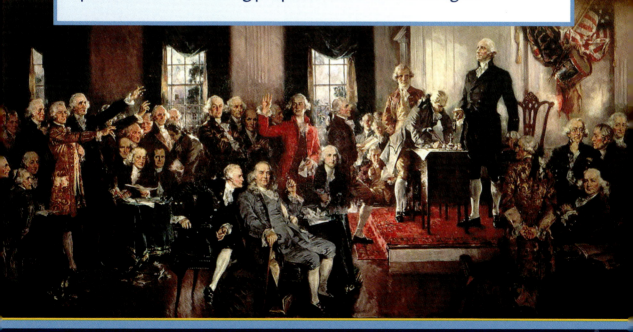

The Three Branches of U.S. Government

The U.S. Constitution set up the three branches of the federal government and laid out their responsibilities. Congress is the legislative branch. The president is head of the executive branch. The Supreme Court is the head of the judicial branch.

Congress is bicameral, or divided into two parts, or chambers— the Senate and the House of Representatives. Each state has two senators, who each serve six years in office. The number of members of the House of Representatives is **determined** by the population of each state, and members serve a two-year term. Members of Congress don't have a limit on how many terms they may serve. The president, however, serves a four-year term of office and may only serve two terms. The Supreme Court is the highest court in the United States. Once on the bench, Supreme Court justices serve for life. They're expected to review the fairness of laws dealing with the U.S. Constitution and decide cases involving states' rights.

> The U.S. Constitution set up a system of checks and balances, allowing each branch to amend or veto acts of another branch so that no one branch had too much power.

CHECKS AND BALANCES

Congress approves each Supreme Court justice appointment.

The Supreme Court can declare laws unconstitutional.

Judicial Branch
Supreme Court

The president appoints justices to the Supreme Court.

The Supreme Court can declare presidential actions unconstitutional.

Legislative Branch
Congress

The president can veto, or reject, bills created in Congress.

Congress can override a presidential veto if two-thirds approve a bill.

Executive Branch
President

WHAT IS FEDERALISM?

The U.S. Constitution was designed for power to be shared between the federal and state governments. This keeps the national government from having too much power over the states. This is known as federalism. However, federalism does not mean the equal sharing of power. The U.S. Constitution has more influence over our country than state and local governments. National politicians have the power to create one **currency** for the entire country. Also, only the federal government has the ability to interact with **foreign** countries when signing treaties or declaring war.

Only the federal government can control our national currency.

State and local governments have responsibilities to their citizens as well. State governments decide things such as the requirements for **licenses** to drive, marry, and own guns. Public roads and schools are created and maintained by state and local governments.

Federalism is a way to unite a group of states or smaller areas under one political system, while still keeping them somewhat independent.

Concurrent powers are powers shared between the national and state levels of government. Both the federal and state governments can make and enforce laws, including tax laws. Both can also make decisions on how to spend tax money on public services. Courts are created on both the federal and state levels. If you're accused of breaking a federal law, you would appear before a U.S. District Court judge. If you were accused of breaking a state or local law, such as speeding, you would appear before a state or local judge. Roads are built and maintained by both national and state authorities.

Federalism is an important part of our government. Citizens have a greater opportunity to be involved in their government and their individual rights are better protected when there are many levels of government. This idea is reflected within states as well. It's an important part of the Texas government.

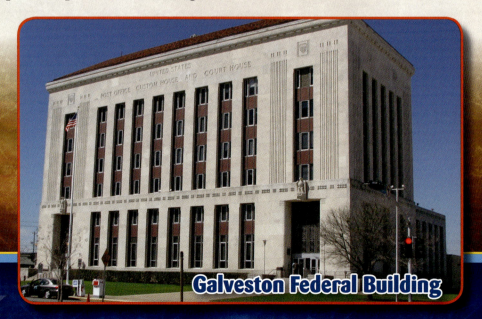

Galveston Federal Building

FEDERALISM

Five Powers Given to the Federal Government

- oversee trade between states and countries
- print money
- declare war
- raise and support an army
- admit new states

Five Powers Given to State Governments

- conduct elections
- create and maintain schools
- create local governments
- oversee business within the state
- ratify constitutional amendments

Five Concurrent Powers

- collect taxes
- create courts
- build roads
- create banks
- borrow money

THE HISTORY OF THE TEXAS CONSTITUTION

States also have constitutions of their own. The current Texas Constitution was adopted on February 15, 1876. After the American Civil War, the nation entered a period of rebuilding called **Reconstruction**. All former **Confederate** states, including Texas, had to rewrite their constitutions to become part of the United States again. In 1869, Texas ratified a constitution that created a strong central government. This forced Texans to accept changes after the Civil War, including granting rights to former slaves.

In August 1875, representatives met to create a new constitution for Texas. Power was given back to local governments, and Texans were given more say in their government. In 1876, the Texas Constitution had 289 sections. Today, the document has grown to include 385 sections. Every two years, the state government suggests ideas for amendments for Texans to vote on. There are currently 474 amendments to the Texas Constitution!

Edmund Davis

George W. Bush

Rick Perry

Many Texans felt Governor Edmund Davis had too much power during Reconstruction. The state's constitution was changed in 1876 to weaken the powers of future governors, such as George W. Bush and Rick Perry.

The Texas Bill of Rights

The citizens of Texas are guaranteed 31 individual rights in addition to those written in the U.S. Bill of Rights. These appear at the beginning of the Texas Constitution. Many points in the Texas Bill of Rights are similar to points in the U.S. Bill of Rights, such as freedom of the press and assembly, as well as protection from illegal searches and **seizures**.

However, some rights granted to Texans by their constitution are different from the rights granted by the U.S. Constitution. Many Texans disliked the strong central governments they had to accept during Reconstruction, so many of the additional rights stated in the Texas Constitution were written to limit the power of the state government. The Texas Bill of Rights states that power comes from the people, so they should have a real say in their government. They have the power to change or even put an end to their current government as they see fit.

> The Texas Bill of Rights includes 11 sections about the rights of people accused of a crime.

FEDERALISM IN TEXAS

Just as the federal government has limited control over the Texas government, the state government in Texas has limited power over local governments. Texas has 254 counties, the largest number of any of the 50 states. Each county elects one judge and four commissioners to their Commissioners Court. This court is not actually part of the judicial branch; it's the overall legislative body for a Texas county. The five members of each Commissioners Court are elected for four years.

Local governments in Texas may be either general law or home rule. General-law governments exist in towns with fewer than 5,000 people. They can only act according to the state constitution and government. Home-rule governments exist mostly in larger cities. They can pass new laws unless the state government declares those laws to be forbidden.

> Dallas is a Texas city with a population far above 5,000 people. That means it's controlled by a home-rule government.

Dallas

TAXES AND EDUCATION

The Texas comptroller's office collects over 60 different types of fees and taxes, including local sales taxes. The money is spent on public services, such as police and fire departments, garbage collection, and public schools.

The 1876 Texas Constitution established a system for funding public schools that's still used today. Public schools in Texas are funded by various taxes, but the burden on taxpayers is eased by a Permanent School Fund. This fund takes money from fuel taxes and land sales, and distributes it to Texas school districts throughout the year. The Texas Constitution states that the amount of money a school district receives should be determined by the average school attendance in the district.

The Texas Constitution also established a Permanent University Fund. This distributes money to colleges in the University of Texas and Texas A&M University systems.

Funding for education was an important part of the Texas Constitution when it was written in 1876, and it continues to be an important part of the constitution today.

University of Texas at Austin

GEORGE WASHINGTON

Branches of the Texas Government

    The Texas Constitution set up a state government with three branches that are very similar to the branches of the federal government. The state legislature is the lawmaking branch. The governor is the leader of the executive branch. The judicial branch of the Texas government is made up of many levels of state courts.

    The legislative branch of the Texas government is bicameral, just like the legislative branch of the federal government. It includes the Texas Senate and the Texas House of Representatives. The state senate is led by the lieutenant governor, just as the vice president leads the U.S. Senate. There are 31 Texas state senators, each serving a four-year term in office. There are 150 members of the Texas House of Representatives, and each member serves a two-year term. The Speaker of the House is the leader of the Texas House of Representatives.

In 2003, David Dewhurst became the lieutenant governor of Texas and the leader of the Texas Senate. A lieutenant governor is also second in command after the governor in a state's executive branch.

The Texas House and Senate have similar responsibilities. Both parts of the Texas legislature pass laws to help protect and serve citizens of Texas. An idea for a bill may start in either the Texas House of Representatives or Senate unless it involves collecting or spending state money. These kinds of bills must begin in the House. Members of the Texas legislature can also propose constitutional amendments to meet the changing needs of the people.

Members of both parts of the legislature can be elected to an unlimited number of terms. They only meet every two years, so they often hold other jobs as well. The legislature meets so infrequently because the creators of the Constitution of 1876 believed it would help keep the state government from becoming too powerful.

Senate chamber in Texas State Capitol

The Texas legislature is known as a biennial legislature because it only meets every two years. Montana, Nevada, and North Dakota also have biennial legislatures.

The governor is the head of the Texas executive branch. He or she is the leader of the state and is in charge of making sure laws are enforced. Before a bill becomes a law, a governor must sign it. Otherwise, he or she can veto the bill in the same way a president can veto a federal bill.

The judicial branch of the Texas government interprets the laws. The Texas Constitution set up the state's court system, and it calls for the legislature to create other courts as they are needed. The Texas state court system has many different levels. The Texas Supreme Court and the Court of Criminal Appeals are the highest courts in the state. The Court of Criminal Appeals hears criminal cases. The Texas Supreme Court decides civil cases and those involving children. Underneath these courts are the district courts, county courts, and justices of the peace.

Texas Supreme Court

Plural Executive Branch

When compared to the president and chief executives of other states, the Texas governor occupies a "weak" office. He or she has less power than other governors. This was designed intentionally after the Civil War. During Reconstruction, the governor was given a lot of power, but most Texans didn't agree with how he used it. When the current Texas Constitution was adopted in 1876, power over areas such as the legal system, state **budget** and finances, education, transportation, agriculture, and land development was given to other elected state officials instead of the governor. This is known as a plural executive branch.

Rick Perry

President Barack Obama

Rick Perry became governor of Texas in 2000. The governor works with both the Texas legislature and state courts through a system of checks and balances similar to those in the federal government.

A Lasting Constitution

The Texas Constitution and the U.S. Constitution are similar in very important ways. They both set up governments with three branches and a system of checks and balances to keep one branch from becoming too powerful. They divide power between a central government and smaller governments to reflect the idea of federalism. They also reflect the principles of republicanism and popular sovereignty upon which our nation was founded.

These two documents also have important differences. The Texas Constitution was written as a response to federal and state governments that many feared were becoming too strong after the Civil War. As such, more power was shared and the central government was weakened.

The Texas Constitution continues to serve as the foundation of the Texas government today. You can see the constitution at work in the passing of important laws, the protection of Texans' rights, and even the funding for Texan schools.

The Texas Constitution reflects the values of the U.S. Constitution in a way that best serves the citizens of Texas.

READER RESPONSE PROJECTS

- Imagine that you're a member of one of the three branches of the Texas government. Using the information you learned in this book and through any additional sources, write a story about an average day in your life as a member of the government. Be sure to state which branch you work for, which role you have within that branch, and what your duties and responsibilities are.

- Use the Internet and other sources to research the Texas constitutions that were written before 1876. Create a poster in which you compare and contrast these constitutions. Be sure to compare and contrast them with the Constitution of 1876 as well.

- Create a constitution for your classroom or your school. Be sure to include laws that must be followed, and be sure to set up a system of government to make sure those laws are carried out properly. Begin the constitution with a bill of rights.

GLOSSARY

budget (BUH-juht) A plan for keeping track of money.

Confederate (kuhn-FEH-duh-ruht) Having to do with the Southern states during the American Civil War.

currency (KUHR-uhn-see) Money.

delegate (DEH-lih-guht) A person with power to act for another.

determine (dih-TUHR-muhn) To decide finally and without question.

enforce (ihn-FOHRS) To make people obey.

foreign (FOHR-uhn) From a place outside of a country, especially one's own country.

legislature (LEH-juhs-lay-chur) An organized body of persons having the power to make laws.

license (LY-suhns) An official paper giving someone the right to do something.

Reconstruction (re-kuhn-STRUHK-shun) The period after the Civil War when Southern state governments were reorganized by the federal government and the states were readmitted to the Union.

ratify (RAA-tuh-fy) To give legal or official approval to something.

seizure (SEE-zhuhr) The act of taking something by force.

INDEX

Due to the changing nature of Internet links, the Rosen Publishing Group, Inc., has developed an online list of websites related to the subject of this book. This site is updated regularly. Please use this link to access the list: **http://www.powerkidslinks.com/sot/tcon/**